To M, G and I.

Always roar loud, my wild ones.

First published in Great Britain in 2022 by Andersen Press Ltd.,
20 Vauxhall Bridge Road, London SW1V 2SA, UK
Vijverlaan 48, 3062 HL Rotterdam, Nederland

Printed and bound in China.
1 3 5 7 9 10 8 6 4 2
British Library Cataloguing in Publication Data available.
ISBN 978 1 83913 154 7

MIX
Paper from responsible sources
FSC® C104723

# HEDGE LION

Robyn Wilson-Owen

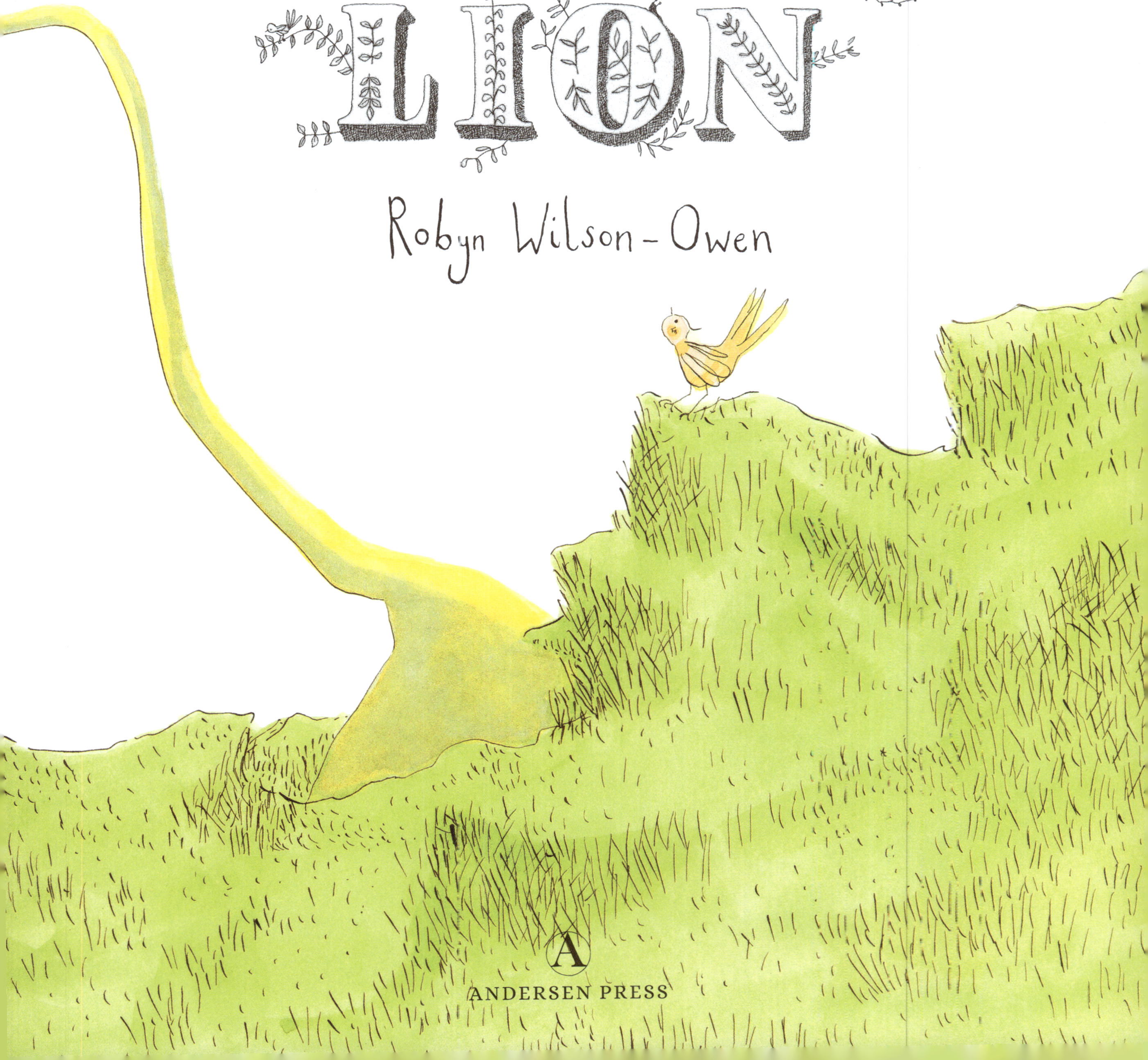

ANDERSEN PRESS

This is the busy town where a busy girl called Ida lived.
Hedge Lion lived here too, but only Ida noticed him.
Ida noticed lots of things other people didn't.

Every day Ida jumped down the mountain,

swung across the river,

dodged the monster's cave,

and roared straight past
Hedge Lion.

Every day Hedge Lion sat still.
Very still, and very quiet, and very hedgy.
He kept all his roars inside. He wanted the world to see a hedge, not a lion, because no one is scared of hedges.

One day Mum stopped, so Ida stopped.
“Come and play with me, roary lion.”
“I can’t come and play, I’m a hedge.”
“You are not a hedge. Hedges are not furry.”
“Some hedges are.”

"You are not a hedge. Hedges are not warm."
"Some hedges are. Lions roar. I don't. I am a hedge."
"Hedges are not stubborn," grumbled Ida.

That night Ida could not stop
thinking about Hedge Lion.
"I know he's a lion," said Ida.
"I just need to find his roar."

While Mum and Martha were busy with breakfast, Ida made herself a hedgy mane and packed a bag of things to make a lion roary.

Lion food didn't work.

Toys didn't work.

Tickling didn't work.

Exhausted, Ida rested her head on Hedge Lion's tummy, and he started to purr.

She got out her best book and they shared it. The bit where the bear rolled down the hill was funny, and the bit where he got his head stuck in a honeypot was even funnier. Hedge Lion and Ida roared with laughter.

Ida turned the page, but Hedge Lion was still roaring.

She waited, but he couldn't stop.
The roars started to sound sad.

Then they sounded angry.

Then they sounded as though they'd been squashed inside for a long time.

Ida got annoyed.

"Stop NOW!

You need to STOP

and listen to ME!

BE QUIET YOU GRUMPY LION!"

Out came the roar Hedge Lion had kept hidden for the longest time.

It was his **Big Scary Roar.**

It scared Ida. It scared Hedge Lion. It scared the creatures that lived in his mane.

“I’m sorry for shouting,” said Ida quietly. “I’m sorry for scaring everyone. This is why I don’t roar. Now I’m all alone inside my mane and I can’t protect the creatures I love. They’ll never come back now they know I’m a lion.”

Ida thought carefully.
“I think you just made them jump.
They’ll come back. I think, really,
they already noticed you are a lion.”

It took a lot of patience, but Ida sat and quietly told Hedge Lion about all the amazing things in their town. The birds and the insects wanted to be part of her stories too. One by one they came home to Hedge Lion.

These days, you'll always find
Hedge Lion and Ida together,
noticing amazing things,
letting out roars before they
get too big, and looking after
the creatures in Hedge Lion's mane.
And yes, the creatures always
knew he was a lion.

After all, he often roared
gently in his sleep.

MY MAGICAL™

# Sea Unicorn

SPARKLY STICKER ACTIVITY BOOK

Give yourself a sea unicorn sticker when you complete each activity!

This book belongs to

..................................

# Splash under the sea

Sea Unicorn is swimming with his friends! Join in the fun by adding stickers to the picture.

# Mermaid maze

Let's visit Mermaid! Add shell stickers to show Sea Unicorn the way.

# Fishy friends

Sea Unicorn and his friends are playing in the sea. Colour them in and add stickers.

# Odd one out

Which creature is different?
Circle the odd one out in each row.

# Spot the seahorses

How many pink seahorses can you find?
Add a sticker at the bottom
of the page for each one.

# Playing in the sun

Sea Unicorn is visiting his friends on the land. Join in the fun by adding stickers to the picture.

# Magic matching

Follow the lines to discover each sea unicorn's magical friend.

# Pirate party

Draw along the dotted lines, then colour in the ship and add stickers.

# Merry music

The mermaids are putting on a concert for the sea unicorns. Add lots of stickers to complete the picture.

Splash under the sea

Mermaid maze

## Fishy friends

## Spot the seahorses

## Playing in the sun

Pirate party

Merry music

## Message in a bottle

## Rainbow fish

## Buried treasure

## Making magic

## Colourful coral

## Mermaid fun

Reward stickers

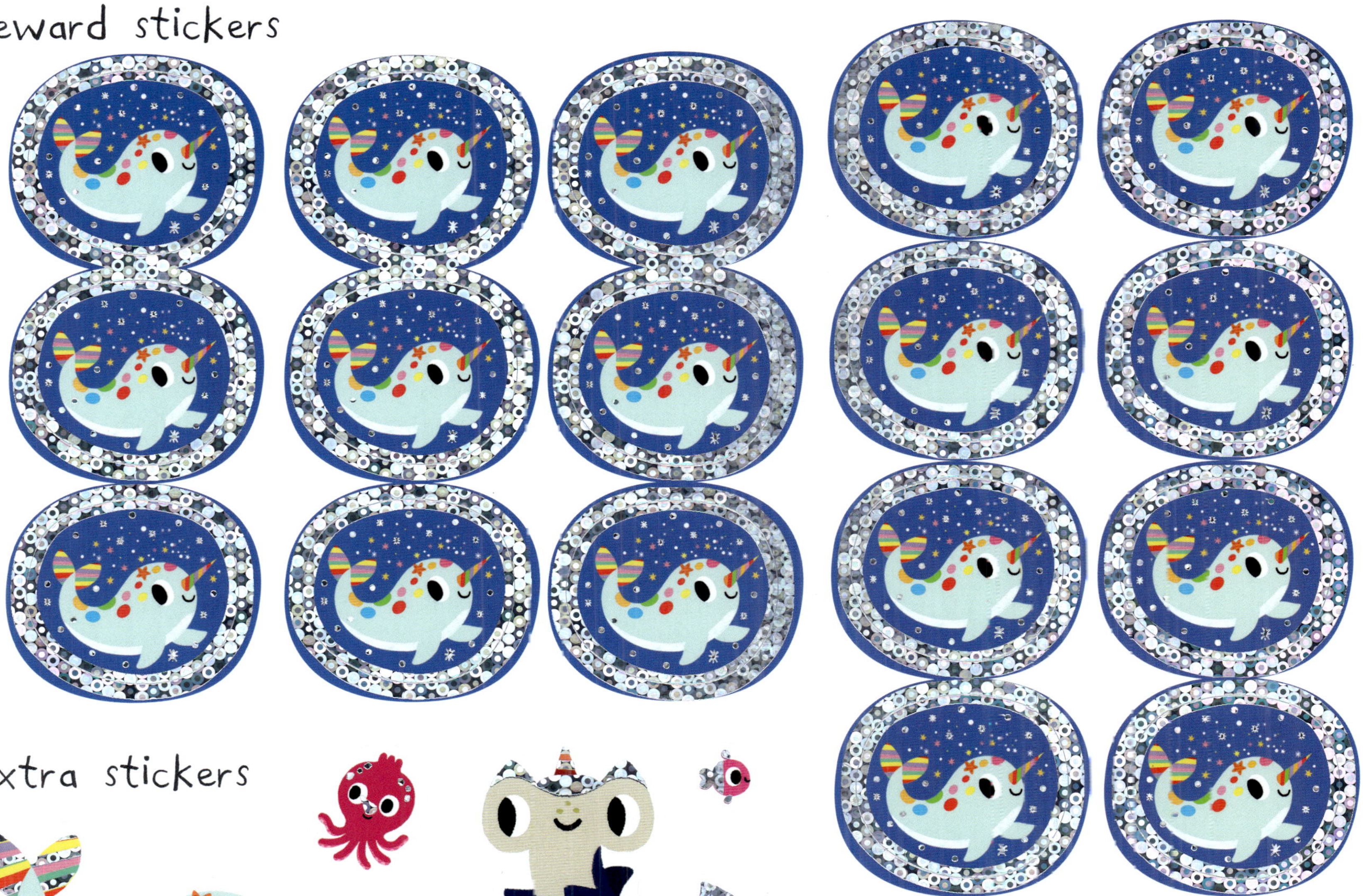

Extra stickers

# Message in a bottle

Add the missing stickers, then help Sea Unicorn find the right path to reach the message in a bottle.

# Rainbow fish

Can you find the fish that match the colours at the bottom of the page? Add a sticker for each one.

yellow    blue    pink    green

# Buried treasure

Help Sea Unicorn find the treasure before the pirates do. Add starfish stickers along the way.

FINISH

# Making magic

Sea Unicorn is using his magical powers!
Add star stickers to make his magic sparkle.

# Sea Unicorn surprise!

Draw along the dotted lines, then colour in happy Sea Unicorn!

# Colourful coral

Sea Unicorn is playing in the coral reef with his friends. Add lots of stickers to finish the picture.

# Mermaid fun

Colour in the mermaids to make them look magical and add stickers.

# Land ahoy!

Can you spot five differences between these two pictures?

# Answers

## Mermaid maze

## Odd one out

## Spot the seahorses

## Magic matching

## Message in a bottle

## Rainbow fish

## Buried treasure

## Land ahoy!